Drug Use and Mental Health

DRUG ADDICTION AND RECOVERY

Drug Use and Mental Health

Michael Centore

SERIES CONSULTANT
SARA BECKER, Ph.D.
Brown University School of Public Health
Warren Alpert Medical School

MASON CREST

Mason Crest
450 Parkway Drive, Suite D
Broomall, PA 19008
www.masoncrest.com

MTM Publishing, Inc.
www.mtmpublishing.com

President: Valerie Tomaselli
Vice President, Book Development: Hilary Poole
Designer: Annemarie Redmond
Copyeditor: Peter Jaskowiak
Editorial Assistant: Andrea St. Aubin

Series ISBN: 978-1-4222-3598-0
Hardback ISBN: 978-1-4222-3601-7
E-Book ISBN: 978-1-4222-8245-8

Library of Congress Cataloging-in-Publication Data
Names: Centore, Michael, 1980- author.
Title: Drug use and mental health / by Michael Centore.
Description: Broomall, PA : Mason Crest, [2017] | Series: Drug addiction and
    recovery | Includes index.
Identifiers: LCCN 2016003947| ISBN 9781422236017 (hardback) | ISBN
    9781422235980 (series) | ISBN 9781422282458 (ebook)
Subjects: LCSH: Drug addicts—Mental health—Juvenile literature. | Dual diagnosis—
    Juvenile literature. | Drug abuse—Juvenile literature. | Mental illness—Juvenile
    literature.
Classification: LCC RC564.3 .C46 2017 | DDC 362.29—dc23
LC record available at http://lccn.loc.gov/2016003947

Printed and bound in the United States of America.

First printing
9 8 7 6 5 4 3 2 1

TABLE OF CONTENTS

Key Icons to Look for:

Words to Understand: These words with their easy-to-understand definitions will increase the reader's understanding of the text, while building vocabulary skills.

Sidebars: This boxed material within the main text allows readers to build knowledge, gain insights, explore possibilities, and broaden their perspectives by weaving together additional information to provide realistic and holistic perspectives.

Research Projects: Readers are pointed toward areas of further inquiry connected to each chapter. Suggestions are provided for projects that encourage deeper research and analysis.

Text-Dependent Questions: These questions send the reader back to the text for more careful attention to the evidence presented there.

Educational Videos: Readers can view videos by scanning our QR codes, providing them with additional educational content to supplement the text. Examples include news coverage, moments in history, speeches, iconic sports moments and much more!

Series Glossary of Key Terms: This back-of-the-book glossary contains terminology used throughout the series. Words found here increase the reader's ability to read and comprehend higher-level books and articles in this field.

SERIES INTRODUCTION

Many adolescents in the United States will experiment with alcohol or other drugs by time they finish high school. According to a 2014 study funded by the National Institute on Drug Abuse, about 27 percent of 8th graders have tried alcohol, 20 percent have tried drugs, and 13 percent have tried cigarettes. By 12th grade, these rates more than double: 66 percent of 12th graders have tried alcohol, 50 percent have tried drugs, and 35 percent have tried cigarettes.

Adolescents who use substances experience an increased risk of a wide range of negative consequences, including physical injury, family conflict, school truancy, legal problems, and sexually transmitted diseases. Higher rates of substance use are also associated with the leading causes of death in this age group: accidents, suicide, and violent crime. Relative to adults, adolescents who experiment with alcohol or other drugs progress more quickly to a full-blown substance use disorder and have more co-occurring mental health problems.

The National Survey on Drug Use and Health (NSDUH) estimated that in 2015 about 1.3 million adolescents between the ages of 12 and 17 (5 percent of adolescents in the United States) met the medical criteria for a substance use disorder. Unfortunately, the vast majority of these

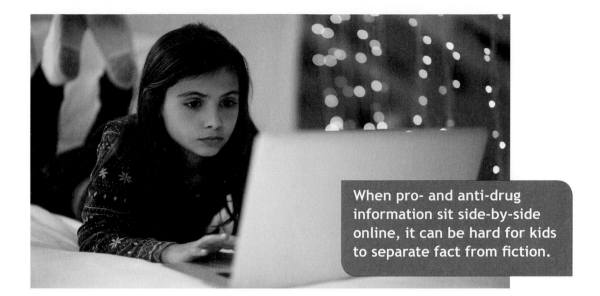

When pro- and anti-drug information sit side-by-side online, it can be hard for kids to separate fact from fiction.

adolescents did not receive treatment. Less than 10 percent of those with a diagnosis received specialty care, leaving 1.2 million adolescents with an unmet need for treatment.

The NSDUH asked the 1.2 million adolescents with untreated substance use disorders why they didn't receive specialty care. Over 95 percent said that they didn't think they needed it. The other 5 percent reported challenges finding quality treatment that was covered by their insurance. Very few treatment providers and agencies offer substance use treatment designed to meet the specific needs of adolescents. Meanwhile, numerous insurance plans have "opted out" of providing coverage for addiction treatment, while others have placed restrictions on what is covered.

Stigma about substance use is another serious problem. We don't call a person with an eating disorder a "food abuser," but we use terms like "drug abuser" to describe individuals with substance use disorders. Even treatment providers often unintentionally use judgmental words, such as describing urine screen results as either "clean" or "dirty." Underlying this language is the idea that a substance use disorder is some kind of moral failing or character flaw, and that people with these disorders deserve blame or punishment for their struggles.

And punish we do. A 2010 report by CASA Columbia found that in the United States, 65 percent of the 2.3 million people in prisons and jails met medical criteria for a substance use disorder, while another 20 percent had histories of substance use disorders, committed their crimes while under the influence of alcohol or drugs, or committed a substance-related crime. Many of these inmates spend decades in prison, but only 11 percent of them receive any treatment during their incarceration. Our society invests significantly more money in punishing individuals with substance use disorders than we do in treating them.

At a basic level, the ways our society approaches drugs and alcohol—declaring a "war on drugs," for example, or telling kids to "Just Say No!"—reflect a misunderstanding about the nature of addiction. The reality is that addiction is a disease that affects all types of people—parents and children, rich and poor, young and old. Substance use disorders stem from a complex interplay of genes, biology, and the environment, much like most physical and mental illnesses.

The way we talk about recovery, using phrases like "kick the habit" or "breaking free," also misses the mark. Substance use disorders are chronic, insidious, and debilitating illnesses. Fortunately, there are a number of effective treatments for substance use disorders. For many patients, however, the road is long and hard. Individuals recovering from substance use disorders can experience horrible withdrawal symptoms, and many will continue to struggle with cravings for alcohol or drugs. It can be a daily struggle to cope with these cravings and stay abstinent. A popular saying at Alcoholics Anonymous (AA) meetings is "one day at a time," because every day of recovery should be respected and celebrated.

There are a lot of incorrect stereotypes about individuals with substance use disorders, and there is a lot of false information about the substances, too. If you do an Internet search on the term "marijuana," for instance, two top hits are a web page by the National Institute on Drug Abuse and a page operated by Weedmaps, a medical and recreational marijuana dispensary. One of these pages publishes scientific information and one publishes pro-marijuana articles. Both pages have a high-quality, professional appearance. If you had never heard of either organization, it would be hard to know which to trust. It can be really difficult for the average person, much less the average teenager, to navigate these waters.

The topics covered in this series were specifically selected to be relevant to teenagers. About half of the volumes cover the types of drugs that they are most likely to hear about or to come in contact with. The other half cover important issues related to alcohol and other drug use (which we refer to as "drug use" in the titles for simplicity). These books cover topics such as the causes of drug use, the influence of drug use on the family, drug use and the legal system, drug use and mental health, and treatment options. Many teens will either have personal experience with these issues or will know someone who does.

This series was written to help young people get the facts about common drugs, substance use disorders, substance-related problems, and recovery. Accurate information can help adolescents to make better decisions. Students who are educated can help each other to better understand the risks and consequences of drug use. Facts also go a long way to reducing the stigma associated with substance use. We tend to fear or avoid things that we don't understand. Knowing the facts can make it easier to support each other. For students who know someone struggling with a substance use disorder, these books can also help them know what to expect. If they are worried about someone, or even about themselves, these books can help to provide some answers and a place to start.

—Sara J. Becker, Ph.D., Assistant Professor (Research), Center for Alcohol and Addictions Studies, Brown University School of Public Health, Assistant Professor (Research), Department of Psychiatry and Human Behavior, Brown University Medical School

WORDS TO UNDERSTAND

compulsive: resulting from an overpowering urge.

depressant: a substance that reduces the effects of arousal or stimulation in the brain.

dual diagnosis: when a person has a substance use disorder and another mental health disorder at the same time.

neurotransmitter: a chemical that transfers information between neurons, the cells that make up the central nervous system.

self-medicate: to use substances to lessen the effects of anxiety, stress, or other mental disorders.

CHAPTER ONE

SUBSTANCES AND MENTAL ILLNESS

Substance use and mental health disorders often go hand in hand. Like the old riddle about "which came first, the chicken or the egg," it can be difficult to determine where the problem began. Sometimes, people with mental health problems turn to substances to **self-medicate**, using drugs or alcohol as a way to cope with their condition. But it's also true that many substance users may experience mental health problems as a result of their use.

What's more, there are many risk factors that are common to both substance use and mental health disorders. In other words, it may not be a "chicken or egg" issue at all, but rather something else that explains *both* the chicken and the egg. For example, if you have a history of either mental health or substance use in your family, come from an unstable home environment, or have experienced trauma, you are at greater risk for both conditions.

It can be very difficult to figure out which came first: the substance use, such as alcoholism, or the mental disorder, such as depression.

DUAL DIAGNOSIS

When a person has both a substance use disorder and a mental health disorder, that person is said to have a **dual diagnosis**. Each condition has its own symptoms that add to a person's difficulties. Plus, both conditions interact with each other and tend to make each other worse. It's a cycle: mental health disorders are usually heightened by substance use, while substance use can provoke the mental health disorder. This is why it is can be hard to diagnose which of a person's problems stems from which condition.

Addiction itself is considered a form of mental illness. Like other mental health disorders, addiction can affect **neurotransmitters** and change the way a person's brain operates. People struggling with addiction may be unable to control their impulses, or they may engage in **compulsive**

WHAT IS A SUBSTANCE USE DISORDER?

A *substance use disorder* is when a person keeps using drugs or alcohol even though the use is causing significant problems. These problems might include damage to physical health, disabilities, or difficulty meeting commitments at work, school, or with family. Some signs of substance use disorders include:

- changes in appetite or sleeping patterns
- unexplained changes in personality or attitude
- a drop in school or work performance
- frequently getting into trouble at school, work, or home
- a decline in personal hygiene or appearance
- a sudden change in friends, favorite hangouts, and hobbies

People with substance use disorders may be embarrassed or unwilling to admit they have a problem. They may also be unaware of the harm they are doing to themselves and those around them.

People with substance use disorders continue their behavior even though their use creates problems in their lives.

behavior, trying to get drugs or alcohol at any cost. These behaviors are found in other mental illnesses as well.

In some cases, mental illnesses aren't diagnosed until the person has already started treatment for a substance use disorder, after the symptoms have become more recognizable. The opposite is also true: a substance use disorder may not be noticed until someone seeks treatment for mental health problems.

PATHS TO DUAL DIAGNOSIS

Everybody is different, but there are a couple of basic ways people can end up with a dual diagnosis. As noted, one path begins with self-medication, when a person with a mental health disorder attempts to mask, numb, or alleviate her mental health symptoms with substances. There are many examples of self-medication. People with social anxiety, or fear of interacting with others, might drink to loosen up. They may feel better at parties, but they may also do and say things that they regret when

The ability to deal with stress can be a factor in both substance use and in certain other problems, such as anxiety disorders.

BIPOLAR DISORDER AND ALCOHOLISM

One form of dual diagnosis is bipolar disorder and alcoholism. Bipolar disorder is characterized by extreme shifts in mood. People with bipolar disorder can shift from intense periods of hyperactivity and high energy to periods of depression, low motivation, and hopelessness. Sometimes people use alcohol during an "up" phase to extend the feeling of well-being, or they use it during a "down" phase to self-medicate against the effects of depression and anxiety. But the alcohol can end up making the symptoms worse, and people can get trapped in a cycle of drinking and mood swings.

Bipolar disorder and alcohol use seem to affect the same brain chemicals. This means that drinking can provoke symptoms of bipolar disorder, as can withdrawal from alcohol.

their inhibitions are down. Feelings of embarrassment and shame the next day can end up making their social anxiety worse. People suffering from schizophrenia, a mental illness that distorts the perception of reality, have a higher rate of tobacco use since nicotine can help them focus. People with panic attacks might self-medicate with Xanax, Valium, or other anti-anxiety pills. And people who feel depressed might self-medicate with amphetamines or other medications that make them feel energetic.

There are a couple problems with self-medication. One is that users can become so dependent on the substance that they end up feeling even worse. Self-medication can thus both intensify the initial symptoms *and* create new problems. Another problem is that alcohol and drugs can have a negative effect on medicines prescribed to treat mental illness. For example, if people use alcohol or other drugs while they are also on antidepressants or mood stabilizers, their medications can become less effective in the long run.

A second path to dual diagnosis is when substance use brings on certain mental health problems. For instance, although people tend to associate alcohol with parties, it is actually a **depressant**. Heavy alcohol use can actually bring about symptoms of depression. Another example is marijuana: pot use in teens is associated with increased risk of paranoia and even schizophrenia in extreme cases. Drugs like crystal meth can have long-lasting effects on the brain, causing depression or irritability that can become a genuine mood disorder.

Substance use in teenagers is especially risky for the development of mental health problems, since young brains are still growing. Drugs can affect the brain systems that control memory, impulse control, and the ability to process information. A disruption of these systems can contribute to mental illness well into adulthood.

Disruptive behavior disorders, *anxiety disorders*, and *mood disorders* are common examples of mental issues that frequently occur with substance use. Disruptive behavior disorders are conditions that involve ongoing patterns of negative, defiant, and hostile behavior; mood disorders are psychological conditions that cause extreme changes in mood; and anxiety disorders are characterized by feelings of nervousness, worry, or fear that distract people from their day-to-day lives. People with mood, anxiety, and some disruptive behavior disorders are about twice as likely to suffer from a substance use disorder. Similarly, those suffering from substance use disorders are about twice as likely to have some type of mood or anxiety disorder. Unfortunately, less than 10 percent of people with a dual diagnosis receive treatment for both conditions, and over 50 percent don't receive any treatment at all.

SHARED RISK FACTORS

A *risk factor* is something that doesn't cause a particular condition, but rather makes someone more vulnerable to it. For example, if older

Data suggest that some teens who smoke pot are more likely to develop certain types of mental disorders, but we are not sure precisely why this is so.

relatives in your family have had cancer, it doesn't necessarily mean that you will get it too—but a family history of cancer is a risk factor for you.

Shared risk factors have a hand in dual diagnosis cases, too. These are factors that can lead to both substance use disorders and mental illness, and they often overlap. Genes and family history play a big part. If family members have struggled with either addiction or mental illness, a person is more likely to be at risk. Some people are genetically wired to have a higher chance of developing one or both conditions. Genes can influence dual diagnoses in a couple of different ways. There are direct ways, such as when a person's genetic makeup causes him to find a certain substance pleasurable. Genes can also play an indirect role in the way they shape

GENDER AND DUAL DIAGNOSIS

Gender is a factor in dual diagnosis cases. The number of men and women with dual diagnoses is about equal, but they tend to have different mental health disorders. Males with a dual diagnosis are more likely to suffer from disorders like schizophrenia, bipolar disorder, or obsessive-compulsive disorder. Females are more likely to suffer from disorders like depression, post-traumatic stress, phobias, or panic attacks. Women with dual diagnosis are also more likely to have been victimized in the past.

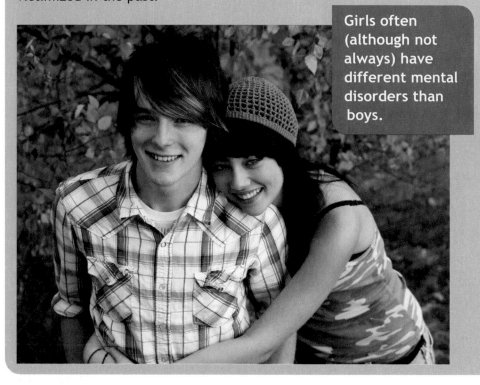

Girls often (although not always) have different mental disorders than boys.

someone's personality. A person who is better able to cope with stress, for instance, may be less likely to develop an anxiety disorder.

Another connection between mental illness and substance use disorders is that they both impact similar regions of the brain, especially parts that regulate responses to stress and risky behavior. This means that the presence of one condition can influence the development of the other. Repeated substance use can affect chemicals in the brain and make it more susceptible to mental illness. If a mental illness is already present, it might make the experience of using substances more pleasurable, which can make it harder to stop using.

Dual diagnosis is also affected by shared environmental factors. A person who is vulnerable to stress is at risk for both substance use disorders and mental health problems. So is a survivor of childhood trauma, or someone who was exposed to drugs or alcohol at a young age. For example, fetal alcohol syndrome (FAS), which occurs when a mother drinks alcohol during pregnancy, can result in increased risk of substance use disorders and mental health disorders such as depression, social anxiety, and attention-deficit hyperactivity disorder (ADHD). Being raised in an unstable home environment can also increase the risk of both substance use and mental health disorders.

TEXT-DEPENDENT QUESTIONS

1. Why is addiction itself considered a form of mental illness?
2. What are some common paths to dual diagnosis?
3. Why is it so hard to tell which condition—the substance use disorder or the mental health disorder—came first?

RESEARCH PROJECT

Research one of the mental illnesses discussed in this chapter. Make a bullet-point list of symptoms of the disorder and how each symptom could lead to or be affected by substance use.

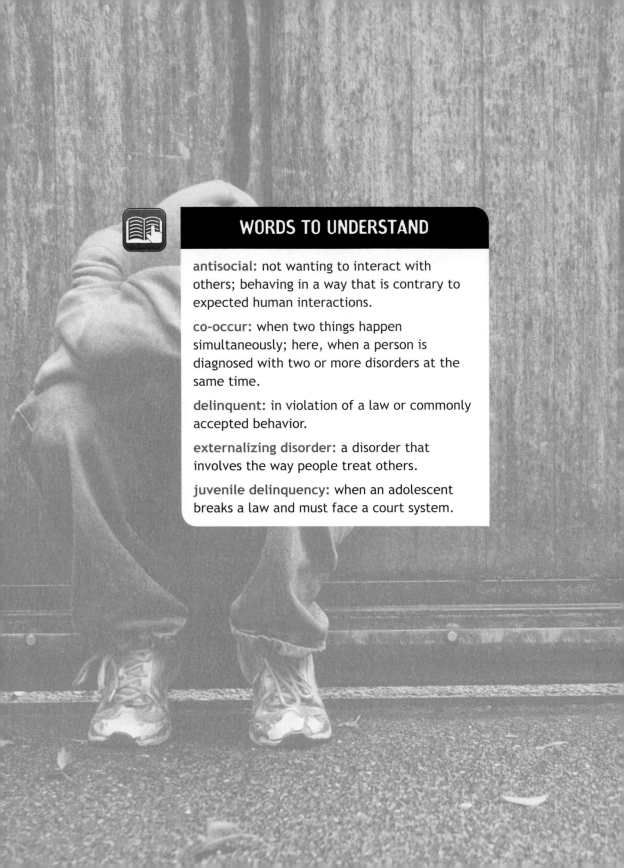

WORDS TO UNDERSTAND

antisocial: not wanting to interact with others; behaving in a way that is contrary to expected human interactions.

co-occur: when two things happen simultaneously; here, when a person is diagnosed with two or more disorders at the same time.

delinquent: in violation of a law or commonly accepted behavior.

externalizing disorder: a disorder that involves the way people treat others.

juvenile delinquency: when an adolescent breaks a law and must face a court system.

CHAPTER TWO

DRUG USE AND "ACTING OUT"

If you've spent any time with young kids, you probably know how hard it is to get them to sit still and pay attention. Kids thrive on motion—running, jumping, playing, and exploring a world that is still new to them. They may throw tantrums, bicker with each other, or challenge their parents. Within reason, all of these things are a natural part of the process of growing up. Kids "test limits" to see what is and what is not socially acceptable, so that they can mature into considerate human beings.

In some cases, however, these tendencies to "act out" happen over and over and cause a lot of distress, both to families and to the kids themselves. At this point it becomes a disorder. The effects of a disorder can last through adolescence and into adulthood. **Externalizing disorders** are any of several behavioral disorders where a person "acts out" in different ways, ranging from arguing and disobeying instructions to purposefully picking fights with others. Children with these disorders may have an inability to focus, control impulses, and stay calm. They are at

Bullying behaviors can be a sign of a conduct disorder.

also at greater risk for problems with the law, especially if they also have a substance use disorder.

SYMPTOMS AND DIFFICULTIES

Some externalizing disorders are called *disruptive behavior disorders*, because they feature a pattern of ongoing hostile or aggressive behavior—usually directed toward authority figures. There are a couple types of disruptive behavior disorders:

- **Conduct disorder** (CD) is when someone has a hard time following rules or respecting other people's rights. It can take many forms, including delinquent acts like bullying, vandalism, or cruelty to animals, as well as stealing or running away from home.
- **Oppositional defiant disorder** (ODD) is when a kid is unable to cooperate with authority figures, often arguing, deliberately disobeying instructions, or blaming others for her mistakes.

More serious delinquent behaviors are usually associated with conduct disorder, and aggressive behaviors with oppositional defiant disorder.

If disruptive behavior disorders continue into adolescence, there is a much greater chance of **juvenile delinquency**. This is especially true for conduct disorder. Children in stressful life situations, such as those suffering from poverty or parental neglect, are especially at risk for this. Long-term risks of an untreated disruptive behavior disorder can include **antisocial** behavior, criminal activity, and jail time. Fortunately, treatment can help those with disruptive behavior disorders.

The condition called *attention-deficit hyperactivity disorder* (ADHD) is also an externalizing disorder, but it is different from disruptive behavior disorders. There are two major types of ADHD symptoms: inattentive and hyperactive. Kids with inattentive symptoms often have trouble paying attention for a long time, while kids with hyperactive symptoms often act impulsively and have trouble standing still. Some kids have both types of problems. Kids with ADHD who act impulsively may seem "disruptive" at times. In fact, CD or ODD can **co-occur** with ADHD. About a third of children with ADHD have also been diagnosed with ODD, and one quarter with CD.

More than 6 million kids under age 17 have been diagnosed with ADHD.

ADHD AND MEDICATION

There are two kinds of medication given for ADHD: stimulants (for example, Ritalin and Adderall) and nonstimulants (such as Strattera or various antidepressants). Different types work best for different people, though research suggests that between 70 and 80 percent of children respond best to stimulants. These medications improve focus and attention, and they limit the impulsive behavior that can make life with ADHD so difficult. The best treatment for ADHD combines these medications with behavioral therapy to help kids learn new skills.

Some people have expressed concern that so many American kids are being medicated for ADHD. Much of their worry is based on the fact that rates of stimulant prescriptions have been increasing rapidly in recent years. But experts have pointed out that increased rates of prescriptions are likely due to better detection of kids with ADHD. In fact, there are strong data suggesting that doctors may be *undertreating* kids with ADHD, not *overtreating* them. The Centers for Disease Control and Prevention (CDC) has noted that many kids who are diagnosed with ADHD are not receiving what doctors consider "best practice" in terms of treatment, which often involves both medication *and* therapy.

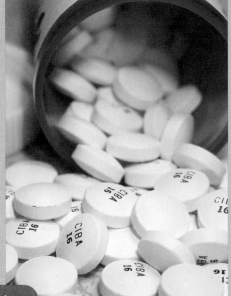

Ritalin 20mg slow-release tablets.

CONNECTION TO SUBSTANCE USE DISORDERS

In adolescents, disruptive behavior disorders often co-occur with substance use disorders. Disruptive behavior disorders can make substance problems worse. Studies have shown that teens with behavior disorders start using substances at an earlier age, use them more frequently, and use them for a longer period of time. Substance use disorders can also increase the chances of a disruptive behavior disorder persisting into adulthood.

There's also a link between ADHD and substance use in both teens and adults. Compared with teens who don't have ADHD, teens who do have it are more likely to experiment with substances at a younger age, which can increase their risk of a substance use disorder as an adult. In fact, adults with a substance use disorder are more likely to have ADHD than adults without a disorder.

The prescription drug Ritalin is often used to treat people with ADHD. The drug increases dopamine levels in the brain, which helps with focus and concentration. What many people don't realize is that Ritalin is very similar to cocaine—the two drugs even have a similar chemical structure. As a result, some people worry that prescribing Ritalin can increase the risk of cocaine use later in life. The argument that Ritalin might be a "gateway" drug to cocaine is supported by research data showing that some Ritalin users have a higher rate of cocaine use than people who were never treated for ADHD. But other researchers have argued that the use of Ritalin can actually reduce the risk of cocaine use later in adulthood. This argument is supported by data showing that kids with untreated ADHD are up to four times more likely to use drugs than other kids. As of now, most data supports the idea that Ritalin use is safe and helpful for kids with ADHD, though more research is needed.

Teens with externalizing disorders are not just at risk of alcohol and drug use. They are also at greater risk of smoking. This is true for all externalizing disorders and especially for ADHD. There are several reasons

Teens with ADHD are more likely to take up smoking, which is a problem because cigarettes are one of the most addictive and damaging drugs around.

SCHOOL STRATEGIES

There are several strategies to help students with ADHD succeed in school. One is to develop a daily report card that tracks different aspects of a student's behavior, such as whether the student has followed classroom rules, listened to teachers, completed assignments on time, and other goals. Points are awarded for good behavior and can be redeemed for daily or weekly rewards—things like dessert after dinner or a trip to the movies. The report card keeps parents and teachers connected, since parents have a steady update of how well their kids are doing.

for this. Smoking tends to run in families, and exposure to nicotine in the womb heightens the chances for ADHD. Nicotine also increases the flow of certain chemicals in the brain that those with ADHD are lacking, so smoking can be a form of self-medication that helps improve concentration and focus. Externalizing disorders are also associated with increased use of several other drugs, including alcohol and marijuana.

TREATMENT STRATEGIES

If ADHD is addressed early on, it can reduce a child's risk of developing a disruptive behavior disorder or a substance use disorder. There are different strategies for treating ADHD. In behavioral therapy, parents or teachers work with kids to try and change their habits by setting schedules, clearing out distractions (like turning the television off when doing homework), or boosting organizational skills. Research shows that kids with ADHD respond much better to positive reinforcement and praise than punishment and criticism. This is why treatment often focuses on rewarding desirable

CELEBRITIES WITH ADHD

Being diagnosed with ADHD in no way limits a person's chances for success. The singers Justin Timberlake and Adam Levine, actors Jim Carrey, Channing Tatum, and Ryan Gosling, and Olympic swimmer Michael Phelps (who has won more Olympic medals than any other athlete) are just a few of the celebrities who have lived—and thrived— with ADHD.

Singer and TV competition judge Adam Levine has been open about his struggle with ADHD.

behavior instead of punishing mistakes. Medication is also a means of treating the disorder (see sidebar, "ADHD and Medication").

Treatment for CD and ODD also involve behavioral therapy. For these conditions, treatment focuses on getting kids to recognize situations that make them angry, learning ways of slowing themselves down (such as taking a few deep breaths) to think before they act, and helping them see that other people's thoughts and feelings matter as much as their own. Treatments that have been shown to work the best typically involve the parent, since it can be hard for the child to change his behavior on his own. Early treatment for ADHD, CD, and ODD is recommended. With treatment at a young age, there is a greater chance for long-term improvement. When symptoms are untreated, the disorder can end up causing more significant difficulties for the person later in life.

TEXT-DEPENDENT QUESTIONS

1. What are the two most common disruptive behavior disorders, and how is ADHD different from disruptive behavior disorders?
2. What are some examples of behavior associated with CD, ODD, and ADHD?
3. List some potential links between ADHD and substance abuse.

RESEARCH PROJECT

Research a public figure who has been diagnosed with ADHD or another externalizing disorder. Write a biographical sketch, being sure to include the ways they coped with their illness and how it might have contributed to their outlook on life.

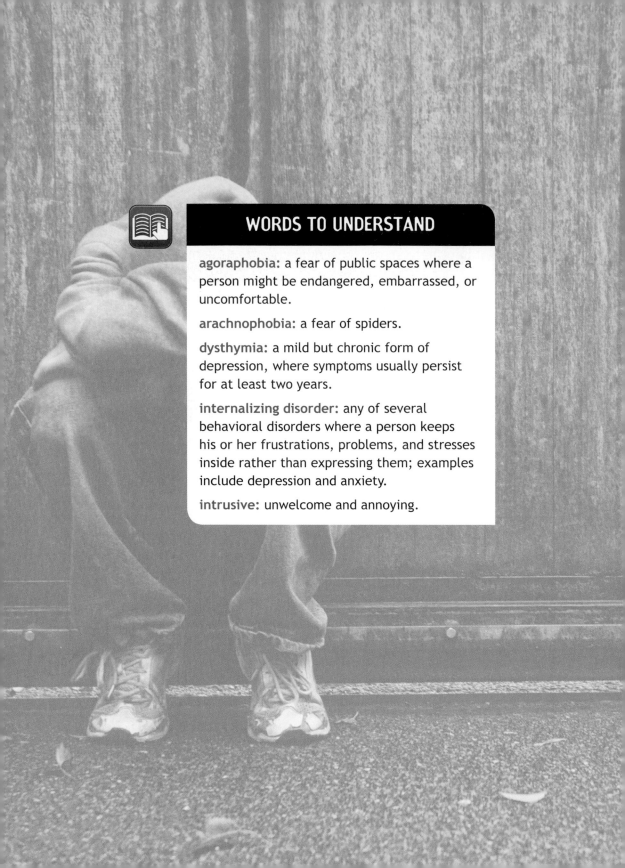

WORDS TO UNDERSTAND

agoraphobia: a fear of public spaces where a person might be endangered, embarrassed, or uncomfortable.

arachnophobia: a fear of spiders.

dysthymia: a mild but chronic form of depression, where symptoms usually persist for at least two years.

internalizing disorder: any of several behavioral disorders where a person keeps his or her frustrations, problems, and stresses inside rather than expressing them; examples include depression and anxiety.

intrusive: unwelcome and annoying.

CHAPTER THREE

DRUG USE AND "ACTING IN"

Teenage substance users are frequently stereotyped as being "rebellious" kids who openly challenge authority, or as hard partiers. These labels are true in some cases. But other kids who have problems with drugs and alcohol are more likely to fly under the radar. Rather than "act out," these teens "act in," keeping their frustrations to themselves instead of seeking help or communicating what's wrong. Depression, anxiety, and social withdrawal are just a few common diagnoses known as **internalizing disorders**. The substance use disorders that co-occur with internalizing disorders are just as serious as those that co-occur with externalizing disorders.

MOOD AND ANXIETY DISORDERS

Internalizing disorders can be hard to detect, particularly in kids, and both parents and teachers, as well as the medical community, can miss the signs. Students with externalizing disorders get attention, since they often involve

According to the Anxiety and Depression Association of America, women are around twice as likely to experience internalizing disorders such as anxiety, depression, panic, and phobias.

others in their negative behavior. Students with internalizing disorders, on the other hand, tend to isolate themselves and withdraw from other people. This makes them harder to notice.

Internalizing disorders fall into two basic camps: *mood disorders* and *anxiety disorders*. The most well-known mood disorder is depression. Depression is more than just a prolonged period of sadness; there are other emotional, physical, and behavioral symptoms that contribute to the condition. Some of these include loss of interest in usual activities, changes in weight, difficulty sleeping, a lack of focus, and feelings of hopelessness. Someone is diagnosed with depression when severe levels of several of these symptoms are present for at least two weeks. Related to depression is **dysthymia**, which is diagnosed when someone has prolonged but less severe feelings of sadness for at least a year. (Bipolar disorder [see chapter one] is another mood disorder that has some similarities to internalizing disorders and some to externalizing disorders.)

Like mood disorders, anxiety disorders have different intensities. Almost everyone has felt "butterflies" before having to make a presentation in class, and occasional feelings of nervousness are normal. People with anxiety disorders live with these feelings every day. Someone with generalized anxiety disorder (GAD) worries constantly, often for six months or longer; this is accompanied by tension, fatigue, and problems concentrating.

Phobias are fears of specific things; agoraphobia, for instance, is the fear of public spaces, while arachnophobia is a fear of spiders. People with phobias experience great stress and anxiety when confronted with the object of their phobia. Social anxiety disorder, otherwise known as social phobia, is an intense fear of engaging with others in social situations.

Another disorder that you may have seen represented on TV or in the movies is panic disorder, which is when someone has reoccurring anxiety attacks. A panic attack may only last a few minutes, but it involves heart palpitations, sweating, difficulty breathing, and other frightening

In 2014 (the most recent year available), more than 11 percent of teens suffered a depressive episode within the previous 12 months. That's almost 3 million teens.

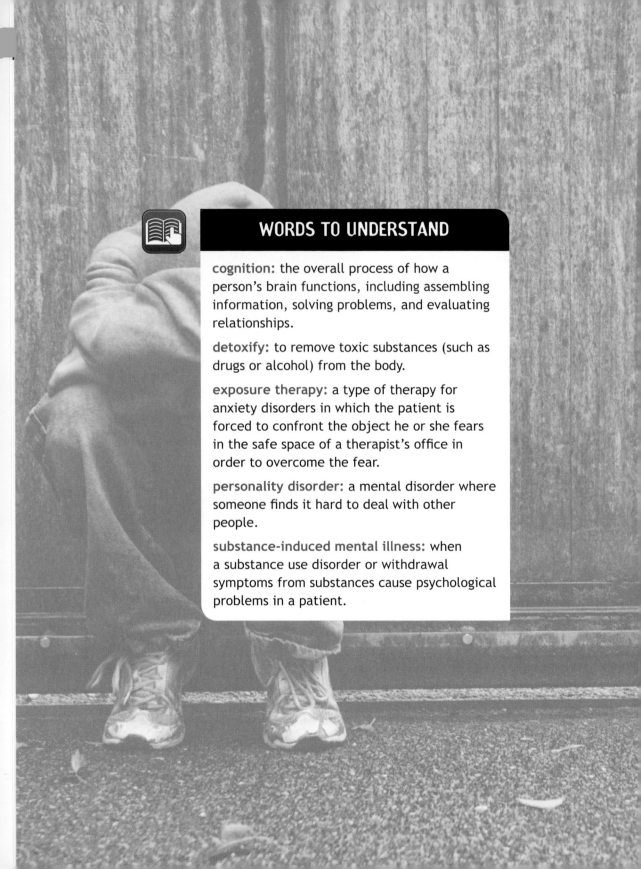

WORDS TO UNDERSTAND

cognition: the overall process of how a person's brain functions, including assembling information, solving problems, and evaluating relationships.

detoxify: to remove toxic substances (such as drugs or alcohol) from the body.

exposure therapy: a type of therapy for anxiety disorders in which the patient is forced to confront the object he or she fears in the safe space of a therapist's office in order to overcome the fear.

personality disorder: a mental disorder where someone finds it hard to deal with other people.

substance-induced mental illness: when a substance use disorder or withdrawal symptoms from substances cause psychological problems in a patient.

CHAPTER FOUR

DIAGNOSIS AND TREATMENT

You can't self-diagnose a mental disorder; that has to be done by a trained psychiatrist, psychologist, social worker, or addiction specialist. You can, however, sense when something is wrong with your mental state and overall well-being. Some signs of a possible substance use disorder include being unable to stop using even when you know you should, seeking out greater and greater quantities of alcohol or drugs, constant feelings of guilt about using, and problems at school, work, or home. Signs of a possible mental health problem include long-term feelings of sadness, unpredictable mood swings, constant anxiety, difficulty concentrating, or thoughts of hurting yourself. These negative emotions can be made worse if you are using substances to cope with them.

If left untreated, dual diagnoses can result in further consequences, including worsening mental illness, physical health problems, and difficulties with family members, teachers, or friends. Adolescents with

A dual diagnosis can only be given by professionals.

untreated co-occurring disorders are at higher risk of legal problems, homelessness, and suicide.

It is important to remember that symptoms of a substance use or mental disorder are not signs of weakness. These disorders are illnesses, and like most illnesses, they're treatable with the correct medical attention. By (a) recognizing there is a problem and (b) seeking medical help, you—or your friends and family—are taking the first step toward healing the condition.

MAKING THE DIAGNOSIS

There is no one treatment plan for a dual diagnosis. Every case is different, and the complexity of overlapping symptoms can challenge even the most experienced specialists. With the most serious addictions, the first order of business is usually to **detoxify** from all substances. In these serious cases, specialists may wait for the patient to be sober before making any diagnoses of serious psychiatric disorders, since withdrawal symptoms can sometimes resemble mental illnesses.

Dual diagnoses fall into one of three types: (1) the use disorder came before the mental illness, (2) the mental illness came before the use disorder, or (3) the two started at the same time. In the first case, repeated substance use may actually lead to mental health problems. The most extreme example of this is called **substance-induced mental illness**, which is when mental health problems are caused directly by substance use or withdrawal. Examples of this are when someone addicted to cocaine develops symptoms of psychosis, or when someone in withdrawal from benzodiazepines experiences hyperactivity, agitation, and anxiety.

The reverse is when a mental illness comes before a use disorder, possibly because someone self-medicates to cope with their symptoms. This can happen with patients who cannot afford prescription medicines for their conditions, and instead substitute alcohol or other drugs. It can also happen when someone with a mental health condition experiments with substances and then starts craving that emotional relief.

In some cases, mental health problems come first, but the problems don't become severe until substances are brought on board. Syd Barrett,

Sometimes people become dependent on prescription drugs and then switch to illegal drugs when their original prescriptions run out or become too expensive.

the founder of the acclaimed rock band Pink Floyd, showed symptoms of schizophrenia in his late teens, but excessive LSD use made the condition much worse. By his early 20s, he could no longer function, and he faded from the music world.

When someone is drinking or using drugs, diagnosing a co-occurring mental health condition can be complex. A medical specialist will usually look at the patient's medical history and past episodes of substance use. This is followed by an interview of the patient, evaluating things like a family history of mental illness, school or work performance, relationships with family members and friends, sleep and eating habits, mood, behavior, memory, and attention span. There may also be some questionnaires or assessments to measure the patient's cognition—the ability to solve problems, use language, recall information, and perform other brain functions. Taken together, these methods help the therapist make an initial determination of the patient's specific condition (or conditions), which could be a personality disorder, an eating disorder, or a mood or anxiety disorder (or a combination of these).

Family therapy can help address some of the underlying relationship issues that could be contributing to substance use problems.

MEDICATIONS AND TREATMENT

Medications are often part of dual-diagnosis treatment. Some substances, like opioids, are so highly addictive that medications are often necessary to help reduce cravings and prevent serious withdrawal symptoms. Medications can also help to treat the underlying mental health symptoms associated with mood and anxiety disorders. Some patients can get frustrated with medications, because they cause side effects and seem to go against the idea of a newfound commitment to sobriety. However, with proper medical oversight, they can help the patient to make long-term changes for the better.

TREATMENT STRATEGIES

Historically, there were a few common approaches to dual diagnosis treatment, known as *sequential*, *partial*, or *parallel* treatment. Treating one disorder first is known as sequential treatment. This ensures the patient is stable in one area before moving on to the next. Partial treatment is when only one of the disorders is addressed. Sometimes this happens when patients are, sadly, denied access to mental health treatment because they are using alcohol or drugs. Unfortunately, this is a common situation, especially if a patient is in trouble with the law or incarcerated. On the other hand, some substance use providers are not comfortable treating, or willing to treat, mental health problems.

In some cases, if patients are using substances to cope with mental health issues, partial treatment that targets the underlying mental health problems may be enough. For example, getting antidepressants or behavioral therapy for depression, exposure therapy for anxiety, or other treatments specifically for mental health problems can be very helpful in combating addiction.

OTHER TYPES OF TESTS

In addition to cognition tests, there are dozens of other tests available to therapists who want to assess a patient's mental condition. Some psychological tests help the therapist get a sense of the patient's personality. The Rorschach inkblot test, one of the most well known (but also dubious) of these tests, asks patients to identify what they see in random patterns of ink. Some believe that patients' answers can reveal things about their personality and thought processes, though the data in support of this test is pretty controversial. Tests for addiction, usually done as an interview paired with biological tests (like a urine or saliva screen), try to determine how severe a person's substance use disorder really is. Finally, some assessments are used to uncover more specific disorders. There are also a number of questionnaires that patients (and even their parents or caregivers) can fill out to screen for specific internalizing and externalizing conditions.

Parallel treatment is when both issues are addressed at the same time but by different medical professionals. This approach is generally recommended over sequential or partial treatment, but all three of these treatment approaches are associated with high levels of relapse.

In recent years, specialists have developed a new approach called *integrated treatment*. This is when both disorders are treated simultaneously, but under one unified program. It has become the preferred method for treating dual diagnosis, because it makes it easier to access care and has better success rates.

Many treatment strategies for adolescents with a dual diagnosis are similar to those for adults. However, it is usually recommended that adolescent treatment involve the family in therapy. Since adolescents typically live with their families, it is important that family members know how to help adolescents deal with the numerous challenges they face. The family can also help encourage coping skills, remove any triggers for substance use from the home, and validate and encourage the teen's progress. (For more, see the volume *Families and Drug Use* in this set.)

No matter what treatment is used, a successful recovery from a dual diagnosis requires the patient to put in a lot of time and effort. He or she will have to adjust life habits, form healthier relationships, and invest significant energy toward staying sober. As a result, many treatment programs specifically work to help increase the patient's motivation to change and help link the patient to ongoing recovery support services.

TEXT-DEPENDENT QUESTIONS

1. What are some symptoms that indicate a person might have a mental illness?
2. Why is it important that the patient detoxify before getting a mental health diagnosis in serious cases of addiction?
3. What two things must treatment address in dual diagnosis?

RESEARCH PROJECT

Research one of the many cognitive, psychological, addiction, or specific disorder tests used by therapists or psychiatrists to evaluate mental and substance use disorders. Write a brief report explaining how the test works, the types of questions used, and how it might help uncover elements of a patient's personality.

WORDS TO UNDERSTAND

binge drinking: consuming a lot of alcohol in a short period of time, usually with the intention of getting drunk.

psychiatric illness: any illness that affects mood, behavior, and patterns of thinking, such as depression or anxiety.

suicidal ideation: thoughts about suicide.

CHAPTER FIVE

SUICIDE AND HOMELESSNESS

The challenges of a dual diagnosis go beyond the daily struggles of mental illness and substance use, which are painful enough on their own. As discussed earlier, both conditions can become so overpowering that people may give up all hope, leading to thoughts—and sometimes acts—of suicide. Mental illness, a substance use problem, and related health difficulties can also make it difficult for a person to find and keep stable housing. Consequently, there is a strong connection between substance abuse, mental illness, and homelessness. *Chronic homelessness* is defined as more than a year of homelessness or at least four experiences of homelessness in a three-year span. Of those experiencing chronic homelessness, approximately 30 percent have a mental illness, and around two-thirds have a substance use disorder or health problem. Not surprisingly, the various issues are interconnected: being homeless greatly increases the risk of suicide.

In downtown Seattle, homeless people wait outside the Union Gospel Mission.

DUAL DIAGNOSIS AND SUICIDE RISK

Suicide claims the lives of over 30,000 people each year in America alone. More people die each year from suicide than from automobile accidents. Suicide is an especially serious problem in children and teenagers. It is the third leading cause of death for 15- to 24-year-olds, and the sixth leading cause of death for 5- to 14-year-olds. In addition, 17 percent of high school students report that they have had **suicidal ideation** over the past year. These thoughts increase the likelihood that someone will actually attempt suicide. There are approximately 25 suicide attempts for every suicide death, and those who survive one attempt are at greater risk to attempt it again.

While things like a family history of suicide or a recent stressful event (like the death of a loved one or the end of a relationship) can increase the risk of suicide, the two most serious risk factors are mental illness and substance use disorder. **Psychiatric illness** is involved in 90 percent of suicides. The most common of these illnesses is depression, which can cause feelings of hopelessness, a loss of interest in usual activities, and chronic feelings of guilt. It is worse when someone is experiencing financial or other difficulties. As we have seen, it can drive a person to alcohol and drugs as a means of escape. But substances only add another level of complexity to the problem, and they usually end up making the depression worse. Since substances can make people more impulsive, those with serious depression and a use disorder may be more likely to harm themselves without thinking about the consequences.

People with a substance use disorder are six times as likely to attempt suicide than those without a substance use disorder. Alcohol poses a special danger: over 20 percent of suicide victims are found to be intoxicated at the time of death, and those with alcohol use disorder are an astounding 60 to 120 times more likely to commit suicide than those without the disorder. Alcohol can greatly impair people's ability to think through the consequences of their actions. This is why many suicide attempts occur after a period of **binge drinking**—consuming a lot of alcohol in a short period of time.

SUICIDE PREVENTION

The first step to prevent suicide is to remove all access to lethal means— like guns, knives, and pills—from the person at risk. Another important step

More than 20,000 Americans commit suicide with firearms every year.

is having friends and family watch for warning signs of suicidal behavior. These may include talking about feeling intense pain or being a burden to others. The person might even speak openly about "having no reason to live." Increased use of alcohol or drugs is also a warning sign, as are reckless behavior and unpredictable mood swings. The warning signs in teenagers are similar to the warning signs in adults, though teens may be more likely to seem irritable or to give away their most prized possessions.

If someone you know is behaving in this way, seek help. Suicide prevention hotlines, such as the National Suicide Prevention Lifeline (1-800-273-TALK), run by the Substance Abuse and Mental Health Services Administration (SAMHSA), can provide guidance in a moment of crisis. If the person is acting irrationally and seems intent on doing harm, it is best to call 911.

Addressing underlying substance use disorders or mental illnesses that might be causing suicidal thoughts is crucial, but it's not easy. People have to see beyond their despair and recognize the larger problem. Many psychiatrists now advocate a more integrated approach to suicide prevention. This means treating the whole person from a young age. It is important to identify risk factors for mental health and substance use disorders early on, and to introduce prevention programs for mental health and substance use problems in places where kids and adolescents spend a lot of time, like pediatrician's offices and schools.

YOU'RE NOT ALONE

If someone you know is having thoughts of suicide or talking openly about it, there are things you can do to help. First, don't wait for your friend to come to you: if you are worried, ask. Try to be calm, compassionate, and nonjudgmental. Don't act shocked or disturbed when someone confides in you—this may only make them want to pull back more. After you've talked, share the issue with a trusted adult or call a suicide crisis hotline such as 1-800-SUICIDE to get professional help. Do not keep the situation a secret, no matter what your friend asks. It is much more important for that person to receive the necessary support.

If you have suicidal thoughts, get help. Find someone to talk to, whether it be a therapist, school counselor, parent, teacher, or friend. You can also call a crisis hotline if you prefer to talk to someone anonymously. Create a "safety plan" that includes the moods and situations that trigger your suicidal thoughts and some things you can do to calm yourself when those moods and situations arise. Even though you might not be feeling very social, try to seek out family and friends anyway. They can offer support and make you feel more connected. You might also read stories of suicide survivors at websites like Attemptsurvivors.com. These narratives can remind you that you are not alone, that hope is ever present, and that help is within reach.

DUAL DIAGNOSIS AND HOMELESSNESS

Homelessness can occur for a variety of reasons. Unemployment, a sudden divorce or family breakdown, a lack of affordable housing, or a natural disaster are all things that can result in homelessness for people in all walks of life, often without warning.

Approximately 610,000 people experience homelessness each night in America alone, and over 250,000 of them have a mental illness or substance use disorder. Substance use does not necessarily *cause* homelessness. For some people, drugs and alcohol are a means of coping with their situation.

People without stable housing face a number of daily dangers, from starvation to harsh weather to crime. For many homeless people, finding food and shelter is understandably a higher priority than getting treatment. But for those who want it, finding free or low-cost treatment can be very difficult. Shelters may offer limited medical services, but these rarely include substance use treatment. When substance treatment services are offered, they are often temporary and do not involve all the steps for a successful recovery. People need to feel stable in order to fully participate in treatment, and stability is impossible without proper housing.

Homeless people suffering from substance use disorders often find it hard to get even overnight housing. Shelters have limited space as it is,

A homeless teenager near Times Square, in New York City.

CATEGORIES OF HOMELESSNESS

There are three main categories of homelessness: (1) *unsheltered* is when a person lives outdoors, on the street, or in an abandoned building; (2) *sheltered* is the use of emergency or "transitional" housing (meaning it helps people move from homelessness into more permanent housing); and (3) *doubled up* or *precariously housed* is when someone stays with friends or family temporarily.

and they often turn away those who are under the influence of alcohol or drugs for the safety of others. Some communities do offer "wet housing," where people can find temporary residence even if they have been drinking. "Low demand" transitional housing models offer a place to stay even if the person has a serious use disorder. Many of these offer services to help people achieve sobriety and transition into more permanent housing. They may not be available in every city, however, and they may have long waiting lists.

TREATMENT OF HOMELESSNESS

In order to really help people, you have to understand how they got into whatever situation they're in. As with suicide prevention, the treatment of homeless patients should be holistic, meaning that it addresses the whole person. A critical first step is to listen to the patient and what she or he wants, rather than trying to create solutions from a distance. More affordable housing would help, but housing does not automatically solve homelessness: the root causes of the problem must be addressed. Substance use and mental illness can feed into problems with keeping a job, conflicts with landlords, issues with family, criminal activity, and other problems that can cause homelessness.

VETERANS' ISSUES

Veterans as a group are particularly vulnerable to homelessness. There are different reasons for this. One is the lasting effect of post-traumatic stress disorder. Veterans who have seen horrific violence might mask their memories with drugs or alcohol, leading to dual diagnosis, isolation, and homelessness. Also, military skills are not always easy to transfer into a civilian workplace, so veterans may find it tough to find and keep jobs. Family and friends may be unable to relate to their situation and provide support.

Fortunately, there are programs in place for homeless vets. Federal funding has increased for veterans' housing programs, many of which follow the Housing First model. The Department of Veterans Affairs (VA) offers health-care services to thousands of vets each year. Nonprofit "veterans helping veterans" groups are also effective, offering substance-free transitional housing for those in need.

A homeless veteran on the streets of Detroit.

Professionals point to "permanent supportive housing" models such as Housing First as the most effective way to reduce homelessness. In the Housing First model, a person is provided housing within a community, and then with the necessary services. This is different from the traditional path from shelters to transitional housing (that might have limits on how long someone can stay) to an independent apartment. According to the Housing First model, housing shouldn't be used as a "reward" for good behavior. Instead, it's the first step in stabilizing peoples' lives so they can begin to care for themselves.

TEXT-DEPENDENT QUESTIONS

1. What are the most serious risk factors for suicide?
2. Why might it be difficult for homeless people with use disorders to secure temporary housing?
3. Describe the concept of the Housing First model as a way of reducing homelessness.

RESEARCH PROJECT

Find a homeless shelter, soup kitchen, or food bank in your area and arrange to volunteer there for an afternoon. Try to interact with members of the staff, other volunteers, and guests of the shelter or kitchen. Write a brief narrative of your experience and the lessons you took away.

FURTHER READING

BOOKS AND ARTICLES

Daley, Dennis C., and Howard B. Moss. *Dual Disorders: Counseling Clients with Chemical Dependency and Mental Illness*. 3rd ed. Center City, MN: Hazelden, 2002.

Hallowell, Edward M., and John J. Ratey. *Driven to Distraction: Recognizing and Coping with Attention Deficit Disorder from Childhood through Adulthood*. New York: Anchor Books, 2011.

Keegan, Kyle, with Howard Moss. *Chasing the High: A Firsthand Account of One Young Person's Experience with Substance Abuse*. New York: Oxford University Press, 2008.

Levine, Mark D., and Mary Brosnahan. "How to Fight Homelessness." *New York Times*, October 19, 2015. http://www.nytimes.com/2015/10/19/opinion/how-to-fight-homelessness.html.

ONLINE

DualDiagnosis.org. http://www.dualdiagnosis.org/.

National Alliance on Mental Illness (NAMI). https://www.nami.org/.

National Alliance to End Homelessness. http://www.endhomelessness.org/.

EDUCATIONAL VIDEOS

Access these videos with your smartphone or use the URLs below to find them online.

 "Dual Diagnosis vs Co-Occurring Disorders in Alcohol and Drug Rehab Treatment Centers," AboutAddiction. "What is the difference in dual diagnosis and co-occurring disorders in the drug and alcohol rehab setting?" https://youtu.be/meBeFAOXTAM

 "The Herren Project and NIDA team up for National Drug Facts Week," National Institute on Drug Abuse. "Recovery Advocate, Chris Herren of the Herren Project and teens from The Park School of Baltimore team up with NIDA to help 'Shatter the Myths' about drugs." https://youtu.be/7LQzLLhB6dU

 "Interview with Dr. Nora Volkow," The Kennedy Forum. "Dr. Nora Volkow, Director of the National Institute on Drug Abuse, is interviewed at the inaugural Kennedy Forum in Boston, MA." https://youtu.be/FSlYyPjY7U0

 "Increased Suicide Risk and Substance Abuse Disorder," healthyplaceblogs. "People with substance abuse disorders are more likely to have attempted suicide in their lifetimes. Debunking Addiction blogger Kira Lesley explains more." https://youtu.be/ikaD5fmRsxM

 "Youth Homelessness—Why?" Youth Against Youth Homelessness. "Every youth deserves a home. Unfortunately, there are barriers to stability, including poverty, mental health issues, addiction, and more." https://youtu.be/w1F-YFBeWmo

SERIES GLOSSARY

abstention: actively choosing to not do something.

acute: something that is intense but lasts a short time.

alienation: a sense of isolation or detachment from a larger group.

alleviate: to lessen or relieve.

binge: doing something to excess.

carcinogenic: something that causes cancer.

chronic: ongoing or recurring.

cognitive: having to do with thought.

compulsion: a desire that is very hard or even impossible to resist.

controlled substance: a drug that is regulated by the government.

coping mechanism: a behavior a person learns or develops in order to manage stress.

craving: a very strong desire for something.

decriminalized: something that is not technically legal but is no longer subject to prosecution.

depressant: a substance that slows particular bodily functions.

detoxify: to remove toxic substances (such as drugs or alcohol) from the body.

ecosystem: a community of living things interacting with their environment.

environment: one's physical, cultural, and social surroundings.

genes: units of inheritance that are passed from parent to child and contain information about specific traits and characteristics.

hallucinate: seeing things that aren't there.

hyperconscious: to be intensely aware of something.

illicit: illegal; forbidden by law or cultural custom.

inhibit: to limit or hold back.

interfamilial: between and among members of a family.

metabolize: the ability of a living organism to chemically change compounds.

neurotransmitter: a chemical substance in the brain.

paraphernalia: the equipment used for producing or ingesting drugs, such as pipes or syringes.

physiological: relating to the way an organism functions.

placebo: a medication that has no physical effect and is used to test whether new drugs actually work.

predisposition: to be more inclined or likely to do something.

prohibition: when something is forbidden by law.

recidivism: a falling back into past behaviors, especially criminal ones.

recreation: something done for fun or enjoyment.

risk factors: behaviors, traits, or influences that make a person vulnerable to something.

sobriety: the state of refraining from alcohol or drugs.

social learning: a way that people learn behaviors by watching other people.

stimulant: a class of drug that speeds up bodily functions.

stressor: any event, thought, experience, or biological or chemical function that causes a person to feel stress.

synthetic: made by people, often to replicate something that occurs in nature.

tolerance: the state of needing more of a particular substance to achieve the same effect.

traffic: to illegally transport people, drugs, or weapons to sell throughout the world.

withdrawal: the physical and psychological effects that occur when a person with a use disorder suddenly stops using substances.

INDEX

ABOUT THE AUTHOR

Michael Centore is a writer and editor. He has helped produce many titles for a variety of publishers, including memoirs, cookbooks, and educational materials, among others. He has authored several previous volumes for Mason Crest, including titles in the Major Nations in a Global World and North American Natural Resources series. His essays have appeared in the *Los Angeles Review of Books, Killing the Buddha, Mockingbird,* and other print- and web-based publications. He lives in Connecticut.

ABOUT THE ADVISOR

Sara Becker, Ph.D. is a clinical researcher and licensed clinical psychologist specializing in the treatment of adolescents with substance use disorders. She is an Assistant Professor (Research) in the Center for Alcohol and Addictions Studies at the Brown School of Public Health and the Evaluation Director of the New England Addiction Technology Transfer Center. Dr. Becker received her Ph.D. in Clinical Psychology from Duke University and completed her clinical residency at Harvard Medical School's McLean Hospital. She joined the Center for Alcohol and Addictions Studies as a postdoctoral fellow and transitioned to the faculty in 2011. Dr. Becker directs a program of research funded by the National Institute on Drug Abuse that explores novel ways to improve the treatment of adolescents with substance use disorders. She has authored over 30 peer-reviewed publications and book chapters and serves on the Editorial Board of the *Journal of Substance Abuse Treatment*.

PHOTO CREDITS